Stocks to Buy

A simple strategic guide to being on trend every month

Rajendran Selvaraj

Copyright © 2012 Rajendran Selvaraj

All rights reserved.

ISBN: 9781717975171

DEDICATION

To my grandparents and my mentor.

CONTENTS

	Acknowledgments	VI
	Disclaimer	VIII
	Introduction	IX
1	Trend Friend	1
2	Sector ETFs	13
3	Simple Moving Averages	38
4	Stocks to buy every month	61
5	Profit and Loss Thresholds	72
6	The Best Time to Enter and Exit	87
7	It is wise to take a break	91
8	Fifty : Thirty : Twenty (50:30:20)	108
9	A Case Study of (50:30:20) Trades in 2018	111
10	Preparing mentally and emotionally for a better trade	127

ACKNOWLEDGMENTS

In writing this book, I would like to thank all the authors who have written great books about the stock market and investing. They have taught me so much, and I consider them my mentors in the investing and trading arenas. With the help of all these teaching gems, I have been a trader/investor for over a decade. They have helped me not just in becoming a trader, but also in gaining a great deal of general knowledge. These books have taught me many strategies, concepts, and approaches, plus the value of philanthropy and so much more. They made me the author I am today, and I cannot thank them enough.

I will always be indebted to my mentor, V.Ponraj, for helping and guiding me like a friend and a brother.

I would like to thank my manager, Don Schiller, who has supported me, guided me, believed in me, and — most importantly —has provided me with opportunities during these recent, rough times.

Author Dorie Clark and her book *Stand Out: How to Find Your Breakthrough Idea and Build a Following Around It* inspired me a great deal. She was kind enough to reply to my emails when I had questions or needed help. She consistently shares very valuable content with her audience.

Thank you to my editors Ann Robertson, Eugenia Nordskog and my daughter Illakkia for their great efforts to perfect this work.

My brothers, Senthil and Nikhil, are always there for financial support.

My father, Selvaraj, made reading fun for us in our childhood.

Finally, I would like to thank my awesome family: my wife, Selvi, and our kids, Illakkia and Muhil.

Sincere thanks also to finance.yahoo.com, and finviz.com for the charts and data used throughout this book.

DISCLAIMER

This book is intended for educational and informational purposes only. Any trading risks are the responsibility of the reader. As a trader or investor, you should always gather information and strategies from various sources. The methods described in this book are not guaranteed, and the author is not responsible for any capital losses related to the information contained herein. Be a responsible trader and investor by thoroughly researching any financial decisions.

INTRODUCTION

As a trader, investor or beginner, you always have the question, "How can I find the best uptrending momentum stocks every month?" Most of the time it is a complex process. Other times it is quite easy. Even when finding the right stocks is easy, we still want to be sure to make a profit.

Stocks to Buy is a simple strategic guide that anybody can use to find the best-performing stocks in the market.

Stocks to Buy will show you that

- market and sector momentum is your friend; crowd psychology does works.

- sector ETFs are the better choice for diversified and focused trading.

- the sector and stocks leaders on the trend will lead the index as well.

- the simple moving averages chart can be used as a tool to identify the momentum trends.

- every month's uptrending stocks and ETFs can be viewed online, showing their past month's performance.

- profit and loss limits, and the best time of entry and exit, will maximize profit and reduce losses.

- the odds of beating the S&P 500 are high when single-worst month (or week) trades are avoided.

- 50:30:20 is a safe and diversified strategy for getting a better performance than the S&P 500.

- a seasoned, calm mind along with controlled emotions has a higher probability of winning trades than a fussy mind and panic.

By the end of this book, you will have learned how and where to find the best momentum stocks and sector ETFs on a monthly basis and also about the 50:30:20 safe trading strategy.

1. Trend Friend

The market is huge

When you think of the stock market, think of its size and power. That means both in wealth and the number of players in the market.

The number of individual retail traders in the market increases every day. One study showed that at least twenty million people in the USA alone are involved in trading. In today's interconnected world of technology, the number of people participating daily in the market is growing enormously. That includes investment firms, mutual funds, and retail investors from all over the world.

It is very hard to imagine how much money or businesses are flowing through the market every day. As a matter of fact, transactions are taking place every minute and every second. This rapid pace creates many opportunities for business to blossom. It provides an opportunity for creators and innovators to bring their products to the world. However, that is not the end of the story.

However, there is a darker side to the market as well.

The market can also create miserable devastation. When a depression or correction happens, businesses fail; people lose their jobs — and lives. In an "everything is connected" world, negative repercussions don't stop at Wall Street. They have an effect on the world and vise versa.

The market is a maniac

As Ben Graham said, **Mr. Market is manic-depressive.** When in a good mood, the market keeps going and going and gives more and more opportunity. Suddenly, though, its mood can change, and it becomes a wild roller coaster. It swings to bad territory so fast because of its bipolar mentality. It is very hard to predict how Mr. Market will behave, but highly trained and experienced professionals can avoid from the devastation that Mr. Market causes.

As William O'Neil, the founder of IBD, reminds as, *The Market is correct always, don't fight with it.* Yes, the market is a huge, maniacal person, but he is always right.

Crowd psychology

On the other hand, if we ask ourselves, "Why is Mr. Market acting this way?" we learn that it is a science.

Crowd psychology is the study of the behavior of a crowd: how people react as a larger group.

This is particularly important when the crowd is in a hyper or extreme mood.

For example, think of the following two scenarios:

1. When we are at a big party or musical concert, we all get caught up in the excitement. We may not even care about other things that are happening, such as someone not having fun, or someone getting sick from drinking too much. This is very normal; that's how the crowd behaves during an exciting party.

2. When there's a random shooting in a public place or other type of violence in a crowd, people rush to the exits. They're so panicked that they miss the most obvious ways out. People lose their shoes, and even worse, fall down. Some get trampled. Many times, panicked behavior causes more injury than the violence that actually initiated the panic. Again, this is the typical behavior that a crowd faced with a dangerous situation might display.

An internet Note:-

Crowd psychology can be witnessed in many real-world situations. One of the most interesting phenomena is the way in which crowds respond in emergency situations. According to traditional sociological theories, panicked groups of people should be irrational, selfish, and in a primitive survival mode.

Several studies have found the opposite is true. Shockingly, even those people evacuating from the World Trade Center after the terrorist attacks of 9/11 filed out in an orderly way, which saved countless lives.

https://www.bestvalueschools.com/faq/what-is-crowd-psychology/

The market is one, humongous crowd

It makes sense that the market is a gigantic crowd; the members have various backgrounds: from corporate and financial institutions to mutual fund managers, retail investors, traders, and day traders. With the help of today's technologies, each background consists of both a domestic and an international component.

With modernization and improved technology, the market is attracting more and more investors, traders, and day traders.

Technology is not stopping there. *With automation technology, now computers and robots are also playing in the market to trade automatically with strategies ranging from simple price movement to complex algorithms.*

These days, trading automation is available for the bigger institutions. But, as technology gets better and cheaper, this option will soon be available to everyone.

That's what makes the market one enormous crowd.

As stated in the previous section, a large crowd becomes excited or panics very rapidly in a hyper environment.

With trading automation programmed by computers, panic or excitement in the market grows quickly. That's why we see flash crashing.

Some groups in the crowd stay calm and don't react

Some groups or individuals, however, don't panic, even in situations like 9/11.

They are able to stay calm, and find a better way to exit. Some among them not only calm down and find a way to exit; they also help others survive.

More interestingly, some brave groups and individuals will try to bring down those who are causing the violence, and in doing so, they the aid the entire crowd.

As we know from crowd psychology studies, this applies to the stock market crowd as well.

What are the available options?

When there is excitement or panic in throughout the market, there are two options that can give us a better profit (or at least minimize loss):

- **Option 1: Surf along the wave/tide**

When the excitement in the market is in good mood, it is always best to ride along with the wave or tide, so that we can get the best profit from the stocks / ETFs / indexes that we are trading. Because the entire crowd has the same mentality, this can make our trades smoother and better.

But remember...

1. Don't join the party too late: that can hurt badly because of poor trades.

2. Watch for signs of panic or distributions in the crowd: see if any particular sector or major stock is getting hit for no reason.

- **Option 2: Stuck with leader groups**

Watch and go along with leaders/protectors — the leaders know when big waves are coming (or even a tsunami) that could swallow retail traders.

Even when a tsunami is coming and the crowd is getting scared, the tough leaders won't panic, but they also will not stay if there is a terrible forecast. These are warning signs and alerts to watch for as a retail trader.

On the contrary, while the crowd is cheering, the leaders remain cautious, but aren't extremely alert.

ETF can give a safer crowd ride

ETF is an exchange-traded fund that trades stocks on the market everyday. ETFs are traded on the stock exchange just like any other stocks. The price changes throughout the day as stocks are bought and sold in the market. ETFs are easily liquidated, providing a measure of safety.

Why do ETFs makes sense?

ETFs are liquid funds that people buy in order to make safer and better trades and earn a profit. Since ETFs are traded as a collection of all indexes or sectors or industries, mutual and other fund managers usually hedge them with their positions, giving the opportunity for safety.

Even when markets are experiencing a flash crash, the collective liquidation brings it all back to safe territory at the end of the trading day. That proposition gives the opportunity to execute the stop loss on the next day, depending on the market conditions.

More and more managers and traders are going after ETFs, which will result in a demand for growth.

For these reasons, ETFs can give a better trade or investment opportunity.

There is a bull market somewhere

As we saw in the previous section, there will always be exceptional leaders in the crowd. They resist "going south," even when the market is experiencing a bear trend. These leaders may be in a bull market — they are out there all the time, somewhere in the market / world.

These leaders can be a few specific stocks, or an industry, or a sector. They could also be a continental ETF, a county's ETF, an index fund, or a bond.

The leaders resist going down in value and contracting for some time — maybe a month or a quarter or a year— and then they may take a leap into the fast lane, providing a great opportunity to make a profitable trade or investment. They usually show form a pattern in their movement. In the next few chapters, we will see how to spot them with a chart and/or with their monthly, quarterly, and yearly performance.

.

2. Sector ETFs

An **ETF** is an exchange-traded fund that trades all the group stocks in the index on the market. They are traded on a stock exchange like any other corporate stock. They trade at the everyday, real-time price of the stocks in that fund. The price changes throughout the day as stocks are bought and sold in the market. ETFs have a high liquidity.

A **Sector ETF** is an exchange-traded fund that invests in the entire list of stocks on a specific sector of the S&P 500. It gives instant diversification on a particular sector since investors don't need to buy an individual stock or stocks in that sector. They are very attractive since the downside risk of in the short term is lessened. Also, it mimics the entire sector of the market: wide probability swing is reduced since the entire index also has to move through a wide range in such a scenario. On the other hand, when an investor holds a particular stock, the downside risk is much higher on the same day. For instance, when the technology sector is on trend, the investor doesn't need to risk only one or two stocks, but can trade technology ETFs for better profit with diversification. When the technology sector is a good bet on a particular day or month, and a few or all other sectors are sluggish or experiencing a downside, then technology sector ETFs can give an added advantage for a better profit. They give a fine-tuned selection of stocks unlike those in either a broader index fund, or an individual stock.

ETFs give the efficiency factor needed to surf the trend waves and also give the opportunity to find a leader in a particular sector for a specific period of time.

1. Consumer Staples (XLP)

The Consumer Discretionary Select Sector Standard & Poor's depositary receipt (SPDR) Fund tracks a market-cap-weighted index of consumer discretionary sector stocks from the S&P 500 index.

Major Industries
- Auto parts and automobiles
- Broadcast media and entertainment
- Hardware, tools and home building
- Hotel/motel
- Leisure
- Publishing

Major Stocks
- Best Buy Co., Inc.
- Gap Inc.

- Tractor Supply Co.
- Michael Kors Holdings Ltd.
- Chipotle Mexican Grill, Inc.
- PVH Corp
- Expedia Group, Inc.
- Time Warner Inc.
- TJX Companies, Inc.
- Advance Auto Parts, Inc.
- Dollar General Corp

2. Consumer Staples (XLP)

The Consumer Staples Select Sector Standard & Poor's depositary receipt (SPDR) Fund tracks a market-cap-weighted index of consumer staples sector stocks from the S&P 500 index.

Major Industries
- Beverages
- Cosmetics
- Distributions
- Food
- Household
- Tobacco

Major Stocks
- Kroger Co.
- Archer Daniels Midland Co.
- Dr. Pepper Snapple Group
- Church & Dwight Co., Inc.
- Sysco Corp.
- Constellation Brands, Inc.

- Brown-Forman Corp. B
- Conagra Brands, Inc.
- J.M. Smucker Co.

3. Energy (XLE)

The Consumer Discretionary Select Sector Standard & Poor's depositary receipt (SPDR) Fund tracks a market-cap-weighted index of energy sector stocks from the S&P 500 index.

Major Industries
- Oil and gas drilling
- Oil and well equipment and service
- Oil exploration and production

Major Stocks
- Chevron Corp.
- TechnipFMC plc
- Valero Energy Corp.
- Cimarex Energy Co.
- Noble Energy, Inc.
- Newfield Exploration
- Concho Resources Inc.
- EOG Resources, Inc.
- Devon Energy Corp.
- Conoco Phillips

- National Oil well Varco Inc.
- Andeavor
- Apache Corp.

4. Financials (XLF)

The Financials Select Sector Standard & Poor's depositary receipt (SPDR) Fund tracks a market-cap-weighted index of bank, investment, and insurance sector stocks from the S&P 500 index.

Major Industries
- Banks
- Life insurance
- Loans
- Misc. financials

Major Stocks
- JPMorgan Chase & Co.
- Cboe Global Markets, Inc.
- KeyCorp
- Bank of America
- Northern Trust Corp.
- Bright house Financial, Inc.
- Ameri prise Financial, Inc.
- Arthur J. Gallagher & Co.

- Regions Financial Corp.
- Met life, Inc.
- Citigroup Inc.
- American International Group
- Black Rock, Inc.
- The Bank of New York Mellon Corp.
- Marsh & McLennan Companies, Inc.
- State Street Corp.

5. Health Care (XLV)

The Healthcare Select Sector Standard & Poor's depositary receipt (SPDR) Fund tracks a market-cap-weighted index of health care, pharmaceuticals, and health insurance sector stocks from the S&P 500 index.

Major Industries
- Drugs
- Healthcare facilities
- Medical insurance
- Medical equipment
- Managed healthcare

Major Stocks
- Align Technology, Inc.
- Intuitive Surgical, Inc.
- Illumina, Inc.
- Abiomed, Inc.
- Varian Medical Systems, Inc.
- Centene Corp.
- ResMed Inc.
- Edwards Life sciences Corp.

- Regeneron Pharmaceuticals, Inc.
- Envision Healthcare Corp.
- Abbott Laboratories
- Celgene Corp.
- Anthem, Inc.

6. Industrials (XLI)

The Industrial Select Sector Standard & Poor's depositary receipt (SPDR) Fund tracks a market-cap-weighted index of industrials sector stocks from the S&P 500 index.

Major Industries
- Airlines
- Transportation
- Railroads
- Trucking
- Services
- Specialty printing

Major Stocks
- Delta Air Lines
- Waste Management, Inc.
- Robert Half International Inc.
- Expeditors International of Washington, Inc.
- CSX Corporation
- Textron Inc.
- TransDigm Group Inc.

- Cintas Corp.
- J.B. Hunt Transport, Inc.
- United Parcel Service Inc. B
- Verisk Analytics, Inc.
- Union Pacific Corp.
- United Continental Holdings, Inc.
- IHS Markit Ltd.
- FedEx Corp.
- Equifax Inc.

7. Materials (XLB)

The Materials Select Sector Standard & Poor's depositary receipt (SPDR) Fund tracks a market-cap-weighted index of materials sector stocks from the S&P 500 index.

Major Industries
- Aluminum
- Steel
- Chemicals
- Containers
- Paper products
- Gold mining

Major Stocks
- Nucor Corp.
- DowDuPont Inc.
- International Paper
- CF Industries Holdings, Inc.
- Sherwin-Williams Co.
- Albemarle Corp.
- Vulcan Materials Co.
- Martin Marietta Materials

- Mosaic Co.
- FMC Corp.
- Ecolab Inc.
- Lyondell Basell Industries
- Packaging Corp. of America
- Eastman Chemical Co.
- Air Products & Chemicals, Inc.
- Avery Dennison Corp.
- PPG Industries, Inc.

8. Real Estate (XLRE)

The Real Estate Select Sector Standard & Poor's depositary receipt (SPDR) Fund tracks a market-cap-weighted index of real estate sector stocks from the S&P 500 index.

Major Industries
- REIT
- Storage
- Commercial real estate
- Residential real estate
- Industrial real estate
- Healthcare real estate

Major Stocks
- Extra Space Storage Inc.
- CBRE Group, Inc.
- HCP, Inc.
- Equity Residential
- Duke Realty Corp.
- Alexandria Real Estate Equities
- Equinix, Inc.

- Host Hotels & Resorts, Inc.
- Prologis, Inc.
- UDR, Inc.
- Mid-America Apt Communities
- Simon Property Group, Inc. A
- Public Storage
- SBA Communications Corp

9. Technology (XLK)

The Technology Select Sector Standard & Poor's depositary receipt (SPDR) Fund tracks a market-cap-weighted index of technologies and technology service sector stocks from the S&P 500 index.

Major Industries
- Computer systems
- Computer software
- Software and computer services
- Electronics
- Office equipment and supplies
- 3-D printing
- Credit card services

Major Stocks
- Advanced Micro Devices, Inc.
- NetApp, Inc.
- VeriSign, Inc.
- Micron Technology, Inc.
- Broadcom Inc.

- Intuit Inc.
- Akamai Technologies, Inc.
- Seagate Technology PLC
- F5 Networks, Inc.
- Autodesk, Inc.
- Red Hat, Inc.
- Mastercard Inc. A
- Visa, Inc. A
- Paychex, Inc.

10. Utilities (XLU)

The Utilities Select Sector Standard & Poor's depositary receipt (SPDR) Fund tracks a market-cap-weighted index of utilities and telephone sector stocks from the S&P 500 index.

Major Industries
- Electric companies
- Natural gas
- Telephone

Major Stocks
- American Water
- DTE Energy Co.
- Southern Co.
- American Electric Power
- AES Corp.
- NRG Energy, Inc.
- First Energy Corp.
- Next Era Energy, Inc.
- Exelon Corp.

- Public Service Enterprise Group
- Sempra Energy
- Entergy Corp.
- Ameren Corp.
- Xcel Energy Inc.
- NiSource, Inc.
- Alliant Energy Corp.
- CMS Energy Corp.

11. Communication Services (XLC)

As of 2018, a new sector was incorporated, Communication Services Select Sector Standard & Poor's depositary receipt (SPDR) Fund tracks a market-cap-weighted index of entertainment and social media sector stocks from the S&P 500 index.

Major Industries
- Entertainment media
- Social media
- Wireless
- Cable

Major Stocks
- NetFlix, Inc.
- Twitter, Inc.
- Trip Advisor, Inc. A
- Facebook, Inc. A
- Charter Communications, Inc. A
- Activision Blizzard, Inc.
- Omnicom Group

- Interpublic Group Cos
- Electronic Arts
- News Corp A
- CenturyLink, Inc.
- DISH Network Corp. A
- Walt Disney Co.
- AT&T Inc.
- News Corp. B
- Alphabet Inc. C
- Discovery, Inc. A

References

The following links are good references for the stocks in each sector:

1. http://www.sectorspdr.com/sectorspdr/

2. https://seekingalpha.com/etfs-and-funds/etf-tables/sectors

3. Simple Moving Averages

A simple moving average (SMA) is an average price for a specific period of time of the underlying stock. These averages are calculated every day from the past specific number of days or specified range.

For example:

Facebook (ticker symbol: FB) was trading between Aug. 21 and Aug. 30, 2017, as below. All prices in U.S. dollars

08-30-2017 169.92

08-29-2017 168.05

08-28-2017 167.24

08-25-2017 166.32

08-24-2017 167.74

08-23-2017 168.71

RAJENDRAN SELVARAJ

08-22-2017   169.64

08-21-2017   168.00

Add all closing prices (169.92 + 168.05 + 167.24 + 166.32 + 167.74 + 168.71 + 169.64 + 168.00), which gives 1345.62.

For these eight trading days, the total is 1345.62.

Divide that total by 8 (1345.62/8) which equals 168.20.

For the eight trading days (approximately ten calendar days), the simple moving average is 168.20.

This can be calculated for each following day by adding the new last-day closing price, and removing the first-day closing price.

Similarly, we can calculate the moving average for various

groups of time periods for any number of days. This gives us a series of moving average lists.

We all know that, "a picture is worth a thousand words.", so...

After collecting the series of moving averages, they can be placed into a line graph against every day moving prices.

Then the current or every day closing is placed on a different line in the same graph.

Now the graph has two lines, one of the current daily closing price and one moving average closing price.

In this graph, we learn how the stock is performing against the moving average. That graph tells the story of the supply and demand volume matrices data.

That can provide us with buying or selling points.

Usually, the following moving averages are calculated to find the best buying or selling point:

1. 200-day SMA
2. 50-day SMA
3. 21-day SMA
4. 10-day SMA
5. 5-day SMA

Leaders can be signaled by using the charts

As prices go higher and lower, leading (or performing) stocks. Charts can help to identify these trends.

When comparing, look at the market index either DOW or S&P 500 price) against stock's SMA charts. This gives us a better view of how the particular stock is performing compared to the market.

Resources

You can find historical stock prices at https://finance.yahoo.com. This is a free site for everyone.

Go to this site, input the ticker symbol then press "Enter" (or click "Search), and you will get information about the stock. There is a section/tab called "Historical Data" which gives the last twelve months' daily open, low, high, and closing price lists.

You can change the date range by clicking on the date range button and then 'Apply' to get the dates you want.

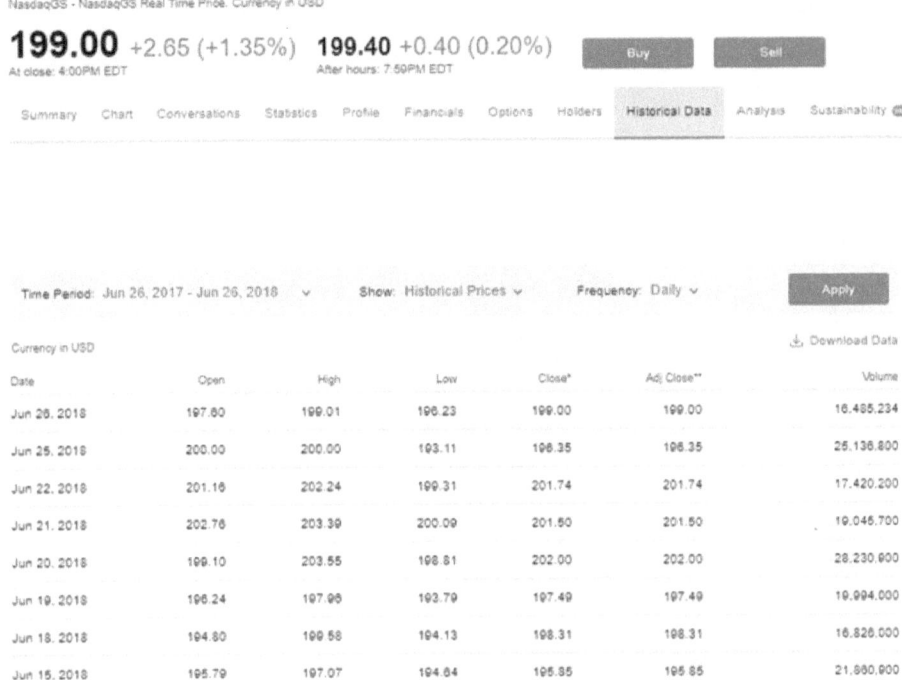

Figure 1: Facebook (FB)'s historical price [Thanks to finance.yahoo.com]

You can also select the "Chart" section/tab on the same line as "Historical Data." This gives the daily closing price line graph.

In that graph, click on the "+ Indicators" link, choose "Moving Average," and then choose the number of days for the moving average to be drawn on the graph.

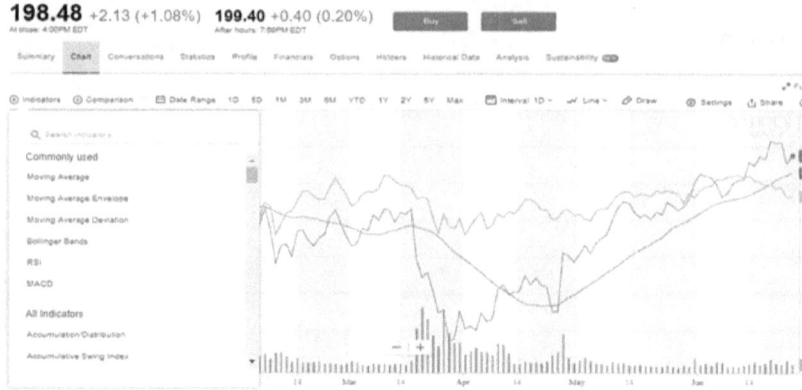

Figure 2: Facebook(FB)'s moving averages chart [Thanks to finance.yahoo.com]

You can also visit the site https://finviz.com/.

This is a premium-based site, but it also offers basic information that is free to everyone.

When you enter the ticker symbol, it draws a simple graph with the moving average. If you want a more advanced version, you can subscribe to the site.

Figure 3: Apple (AAPL)'s moving average chart [Thanks to finviz.com]

200-day SMA

The 200-day SMA signals a more reliable, long-term trend. When the daily price line crosses above the 200-day SMA line, the stock price is ready to go up for an extended period.

This happens when the previous downtrend was longer (i.e., the price line was below the 200-day SMA line for a longer time) and then crossed above the 200-day SMA line.

The reverse also applies. When the daily price goes down on the 200-day SMA line, a downtrend will occur, either for a short time or an extended period.

This will happen when the stock has resisted the buying/selling power for a few months or quarters.

You can also wait for a couple days to see if the up or down trend is continuing. If the price is resisting going up or down, the price trend could reverse.

The chart below shows the Energy Sector ETF (XLE), when the price goes above the 200-day moving average. From the third week of Nov. 2017, the price kept going up until the third week of Jan. 2018.

When the price goes below the 200-day SMA in first week of Feb. 2018, it keeps resisting. And it does it again when it starts going up on the first week of Apr. 2018. This trend continued until Jun. 2018.

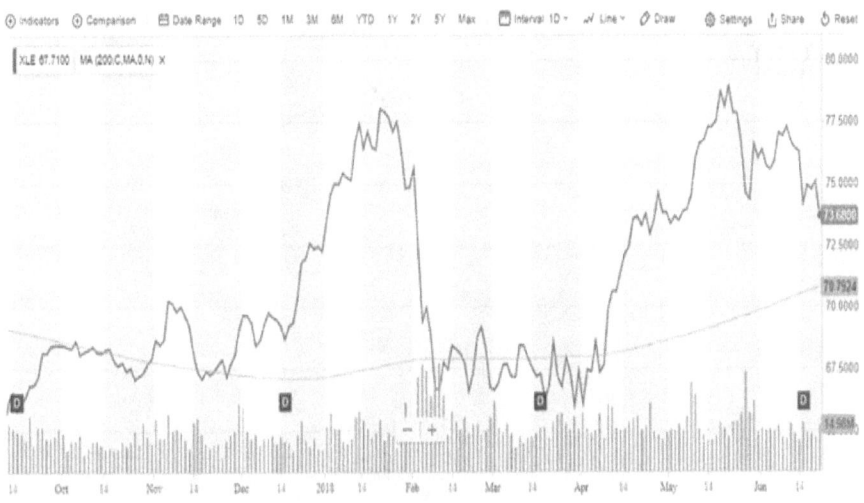

Figure 4: XLE 200-day SMA [Thanks to finance.yahoo.com]

50-day SMA

The 50-day SMA shows the support for a continually moving trend. This will happen when the stock has resisted buying or selling power for months. The better spike signal confirms the long-term trend. When the daily price line crosses above the 50-day moving average line, the stock price will go up for at least a few weeks or months.

Downtrend signals can also be identified by watching the price cross below the 50-day moving average:

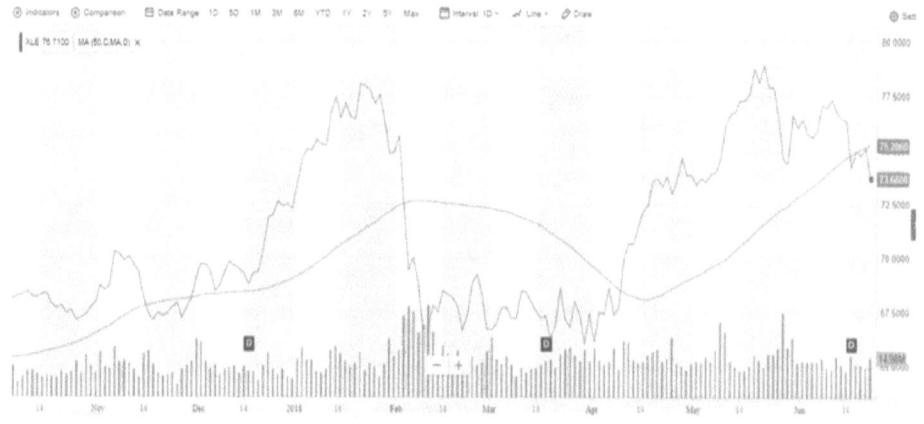

Figure 5: XLE 50-day SMA [Thanks to finance.yahoo.com]

200- and 50-day SMAs

The 50- and 200-day moving averages can help confirm up- or downtrends.

When the 50-day SMA crosses above the 200-day SMA, then there is enough support to continue the trend.

When the price crosses above the 50-day SMA, and the 50-day SMA is above or has crossed over the 200-day SMA, you can make a decision to buy the stock.

If the price is falling below the 50-day SMA, you can decide to sell or reduce your position in order to take a profit and/or avoid losses.

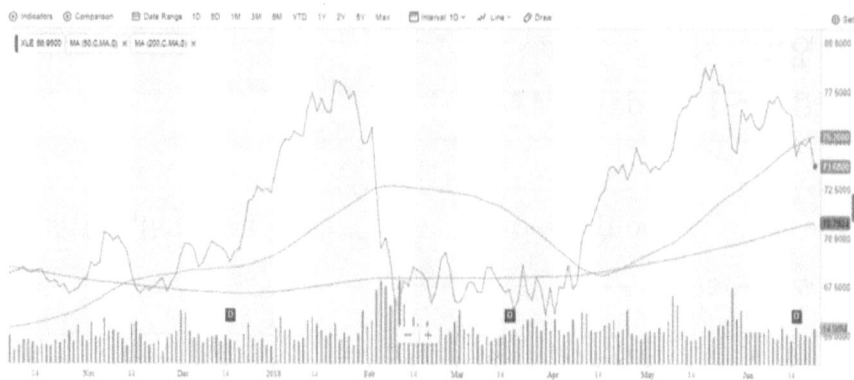

Figure 6: XLE 200 and 50-day SMA [Thanks to finance.yahoo.com]

Comparing against S&P 500

The pricing chart can be combined with other ticker or index symbols for comparison.

You can do this in https://finance.yahoo.com by clicking the "+ Comparison" button on the chart and adding an index.

This comparative analysis provides an opportunity to check how the stock itself and SMAs are performing against the S&P

500 or any other index you want to use for comparison.

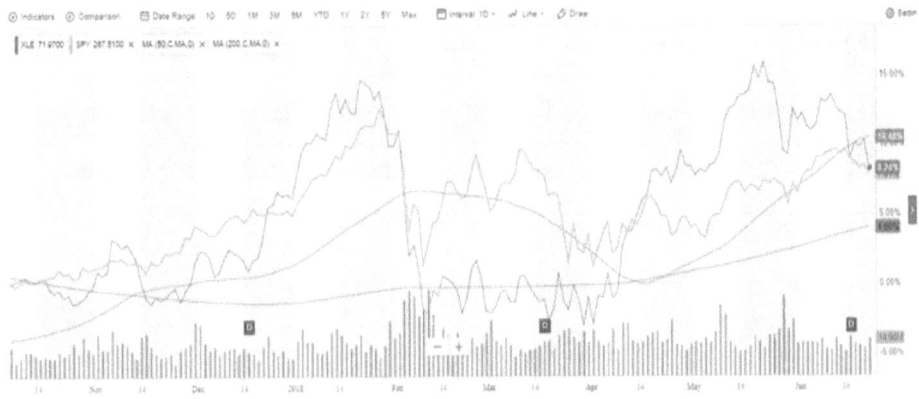

Figure 7: XLE 200 and 50-day SMAs against S&P 500

21-day SMA

The 21-day SMA provides the signal for an intermediate and short-term uptrend. This trend can last days or weeks. Using this chart will make sure that intraday pricing movement will not go below our stop-loss settings.

By carefully analyzing the 21-day SMA uptrend setting, the stop-loss limit scan leverages the profits. The 21-day SMA changes/swings within a day or days on big volatile stocks or market conditions.

The pricing chart can be combined with other ticker or index symbols for comparison.

STOCKS TO BUY

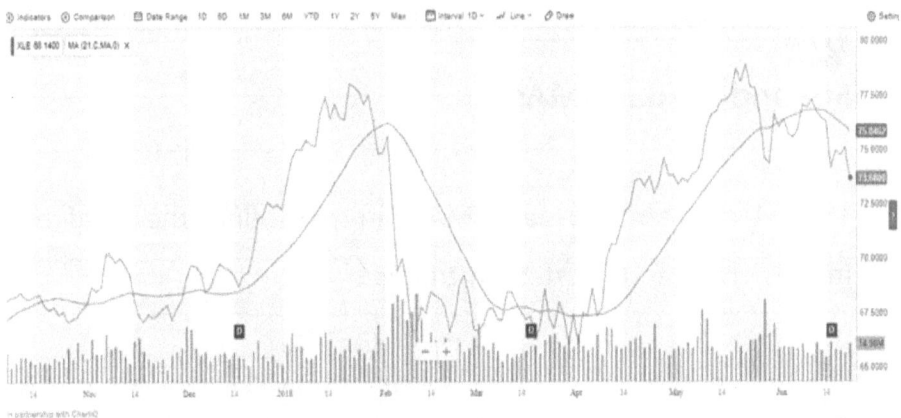

Figure 8: XLE 21-day SMA [Thanks to finance.yahoo.com]

50- and 21-day SMAs

The 21-day and 50-day SMA can help find the confirmed intermediate and short-term trends.

When the 21-day SMA crosses above the 50-day SMA, then there is enough support for the confirmed intermediate uptrend to continue.

When the price crosses above the 21-day SMA, and the 21-day SMA is above or crossed over by the 50-day SMA, you can decide to buy for short-term momentum trading.

If the price falls below the 21-day SMA, you can decide to sell or reduce the position to take a profit and/or avoid losses. Also, this can help set an alert in the trade before it drops further down from the range.

STOCKS TO BUY

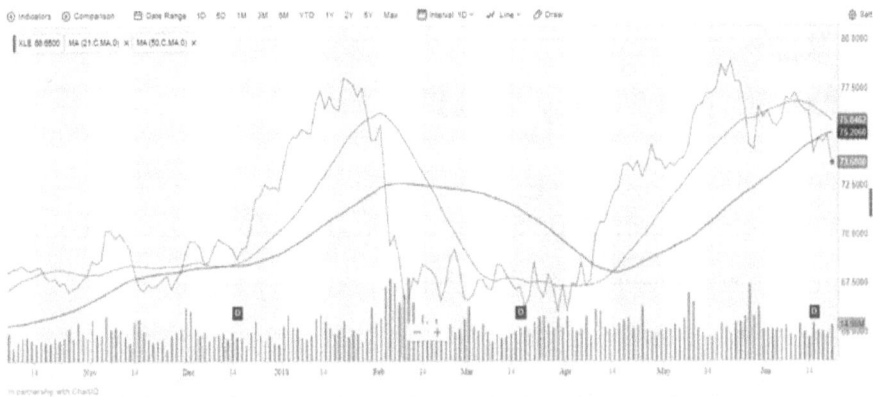

Figure 9: XLE 21 and 50-day SMAs [Thanks to finance.yahoo.com]

200, 50, and 21-day SMAs

When combining 200, 50, and 21-day SMAs we can confirm profitable trade in both the short- and long-term.

If the 21-day SMA crosses above the 50-day SMA, then there is enough support for a confirmed intermediate uptrend.

If the 21-day SMA crosses above the 50-day SMA and the 50-day SMA is above the 200-day SMA, this shows a clear signal for an uptrend.

When these three criteria meet, the odds for a favorable profit trade are high:

1. price has crossed above the 21-day SMA;

2. 21-day SMA is above or has crossed over the 50-day SMA;

3. 50-day SMA is above the 200-day SMA.

While in a confirmed and clear uptrend, you can set the alerts for times when the price goes below the 21-day SMA.

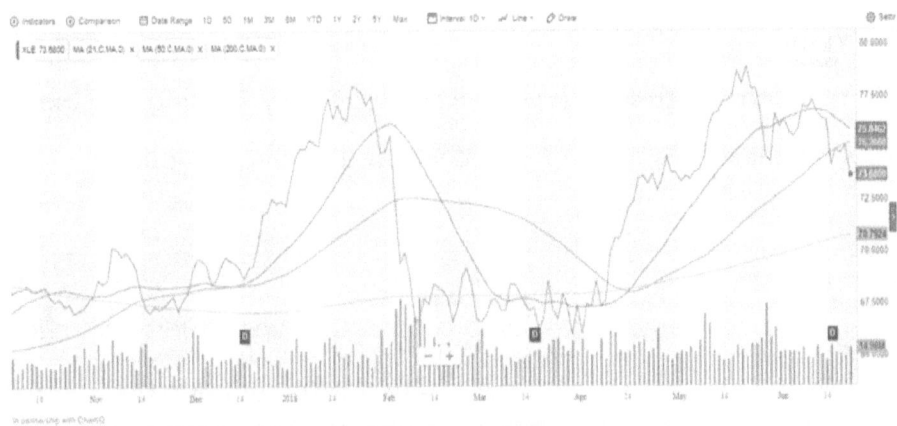

Figure 10: XLE 200, 50 and 21-day SMAs [Thanks to finance.yahoo.com]

Comparing against S&P 500

The pricing chart and all three SMA charts can be combined with other ticker or index symbols for comparison.

You can do this in *finance.yahoo.com* by clicking on the "+ Comparison" button on the chart and adding an index.

This comparative analysis provides the opportunity to check how the stock itself and SMAs are performing against the S&P 500 or another index you want to compare with.

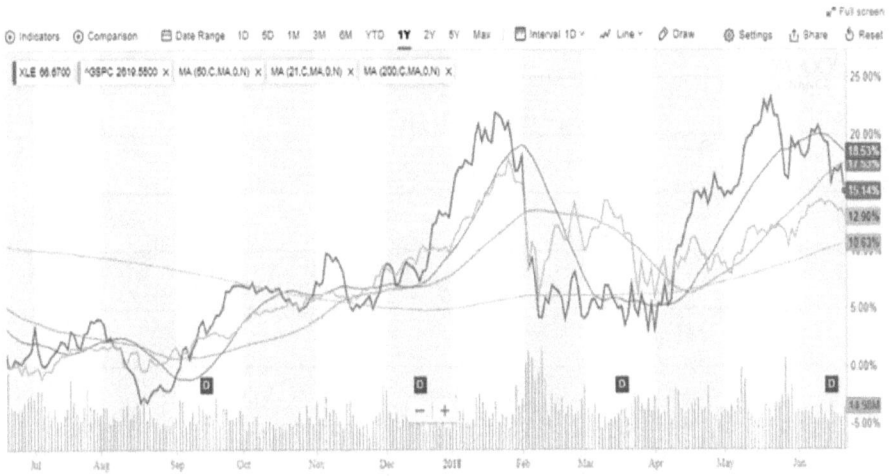

Figure 11: XLE 200, 50 and 21-day SMA compared against the S&P 500 [Thanks to finance.yahoo.com]

4. Stocks to buy every month

As we saw in previous chapters, when their uptrend and momentum is continuing, the value of leader stocks or industries will keep increasing.

1. Diversified and conservative trades

We can find out the **three** leading sectors every month by assessing eleven S&P 500 sectors by their monthly performance. Although it may not reflect positive performance, we can look for the highest low monthly performance rather than wider negative performance.

As we examined in the previous chapters, these sectors also have the highest probability of performing better over the next month.

These trends can be back-tested by their SMA charts, as discussed in Chapter 3.

Take the profits when reaching the benchmark ratio or sell by the end of the month.

We will discuss the profit limit in the next chapter.

Cut your losses with a stop-loss order to avoid a bigger loss. You will learn about stop-loss limits and the best time to buy/sell in the next chapters.

2. Individual Stocks for better profitability, slightly higher-risk trades

- We can find the **five** leading sectors every month by assessing the top five of the eleven S&P 500 sectors by their monthly performance. They may not show positive performance, in which case, we can look for the lowest low negative monthly performance than wider negative performance.

- From the five best performing sectors, we can select the two top stocks in each of the respective sectors.

These stocks will lead that industry or the sector for the upcoming month or part of the next month.

Take the profits as when reach the benchmark ratio or sell by the end of the month.

Cut your losses with a stop-loss order to avoid an even bigger loss.

In the chapters to follow, we will discuss profit and loss limits and times to buy and sell.

How and where to find the best performing stocks?

1. The beginning of the month

On the last day of every month, go to the **SPDR select sector** website to find out the best performing sectors for that month.

http://www.sectorspdr.com/sectorspdr/tools/sector-tracker

- **For diversified and conservative**

Choose the monthly performance, which will show the best performing sectors of the last month.

Select the top three performing sectors to invest in for the next month. In the example for July 2018 top performing sectors are Real Estate (XLRE), Consumer Staples (XLP), and Consumer Discretionary (XLY).

These sectors can be back-tested against the SMA uptrend.

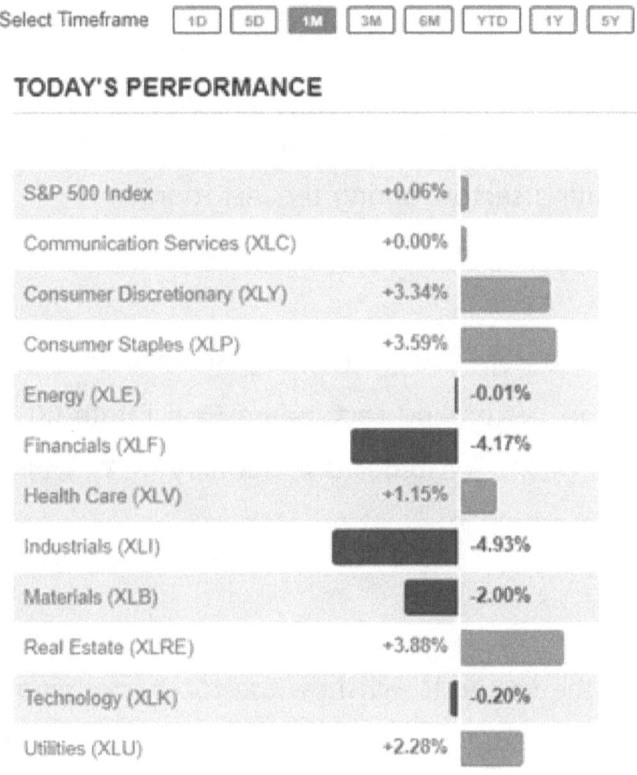

Figure 12: Monthly sectors performance [Thanks to SPDR Select Sector]

o **For Individual Stocks with better profitability, slightly higher risk**

Choose the monthly performance, which will show the best performing sectors during the last month.

Select the top five performing sectors. In the example July 2018 top performing sectors are Real Estate (XLRE), Consumer Staples (XLP), Consumer Discretionary (XLY), Utilities (XLU), and Health Care (XLV).

Select the sector. It will show the top performing stocks in that sector. Choose the top two performing stocks to invest in for that month. In the next example, the top performing stocks in Real Estate are Kimco Realty Corp (KIM) and Equinix, Inc. (EQIX).

Repeat the same procedure for all five sectors.

STOCKS TO BUY

These stocks can be back-tested by comparing them with the uptrend in SMA charts.

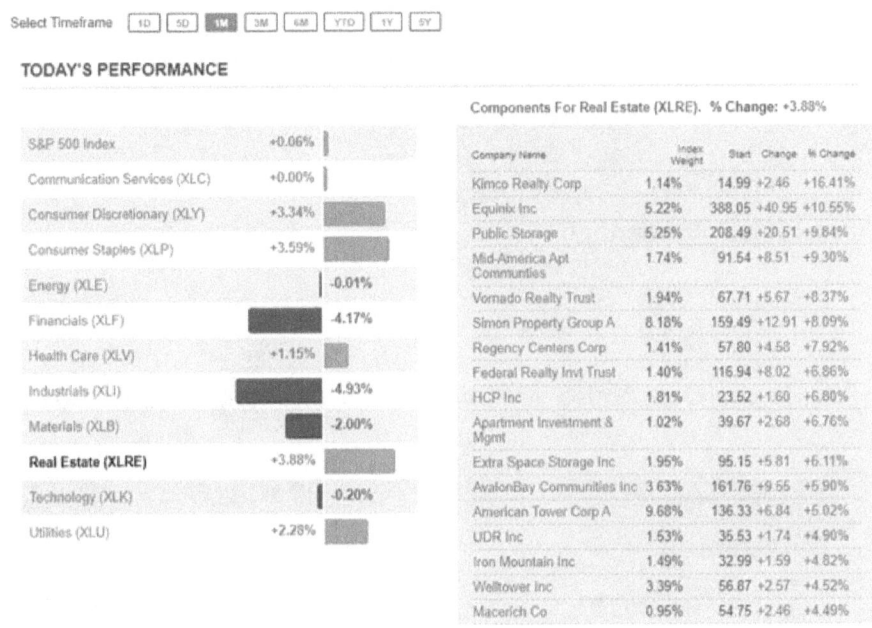

Figure 13: Monthly stock performance [Thanks to SPDR Select Sector]

2. The middle of the month

On the 15th of every month, go to https://finviz.com,

1. Select **Screener**

2. In the Descriptive section, set **Index** filter to **S&P 500**

Figure 14: S&P 500 index filter [Thanks to finviz.com]

3. In the Technical section, select the filters as follows:

- **200-day SMA** – Select **SMA 200 below SMA 50**

- **50-day SMA** – Select **SMA50 below SMA 21**

- **21-day SMA** – select **Price crossed SMA 21 above**

- Can also be adjusted with **Price above SMA 21**.

Figure 15: SMAs technical filter [Thanks to finviz.com]

4. Make sure that the stock sectors you are going to choose are aligned with the SPDR Select Sector's top five performing sectors of that month.

5. These trades can be extended to the 15th of the month instead of the last day of that month, but must be closed by the 15th of the following month.

Taxes and commission fees

If you are making fifteen to twenty trades per month, obviously you will incur many commission fees — not to mention taxes.

But, as *Investors Business Daily* founder William O'Neil wrote, *the taxes and trading commission fees will be very negligible when you are making a consistent profit, or cutting the loss.*

So, don't worry about the commission costs; instead, focus on making a better trade.here. Insert chapter four text here.

5. Profit and Loss Thresholds

Why are profit and loss limits critical?

When did you last participate in a 5K walk or run? What did you want to remember from that run?

Alternatively, think of watching a 100-meter, 1000-meter dash or a marathon. Two things come to mind:

1. What was the distance covered?

2. How much time did it take?

Even if you are doing the 5Kfun run, you won't feel satisfied (and no one will be there to congratulate you) if you reach the finish line eight hours later!

Similarly, you may feel guilty if you only run 1K out of a 5K event.

Put simply: time and distance matter.

In a marathon, the distance is defined, but the time is determined by the runner.

Let's say you're running a marathon, and you declare that there is no limit for the distance and time. If that were the case, then you wouldn't be running a marathon at all.

So, coming back to trading, both time and profit percentages are very important. You should always have a predetermined time and profit goal on any trade.

You could proclaim, "I am not in a race." Instead of racing, you are walking slowly without goals for either time or distance. At some point in time, your feet will bleed or you will become dehydrated, and you will be forced to step out of your walk before you are hospitalized.

If time is not a big factor, it will be the distance that makes you drop out. If you keep going on that track, then death may be the result.

Returning to the topic of trading —a trade should have parameters for both winning, and losing.

Let's picture to a different scenario. In a 5K walk, a person ran 1K in just three minutes, beating all the others. Does that mean he completed the 5K run? No, he might run fast, but he only finished a tiny part of it. Also, there's no guarantee that this person will do as well next time at the same location, and doing the same 5K run, even if it's years later.

A self-help book taught me that life is not a 100-meter dash or a single marathon. Instead it contains many 1,000-meter runs, and so does trading life.

As Warren Buffet says even though you can hit loaded base

home runs when you get chance, but you don't miss single or double as frequent as you can.

Therefore, it is critical to set profit and loss limits for both single trades and multiple trades.

Monthly Profit and Loss limits

1. **When trading on Index** (SPY, QQQ, DIA, etc.)

Buy the SPY or other index ETF on the first day of the month, as described in the next chapter. If there is a 2-3% profit in the first week, take the profit and close the trade. If profit goes up by 5-6% at anytime in the month, take the profit and close the trade.

Set the stop-loss to 5-6% for anytime during that month, and if reached, close the trade and accept the loss.

If none of the above scenarios happen by the end of the month, close the trade by the last day of the month. In other words, when the trade didn't earn 5-6% profit or didn't lose 5% of the capital close the trade by the last day of the month.

If the stock index (SPY, QQQ, DIA) stayed in the same range, and you are buying more than 1000 in quantity, you can just hold onto them for the next month in order to reduce commission costs. In that case, for the next month, consider the starting point of the stock as the first day's price. Meaning, assume that you took the small percentage of profit or loss on the previous month then start the next month with that as the new buying price.

What if the stop loss is higher than the profit range of the first week? If the index drops more than 5%, most likely it will bounce back within the next week.

Why take just 2-3% profit, even within the first week? If the price goes up we more than 2-3% within the first five trading days, most likely it will come down the following week. But you don't want to lose the profit in the short term. This is an opportunity to increase your profit margin. Because our total target trading time is just one month, the 2-3% profit in the first week reduces our average number of days on the trade.

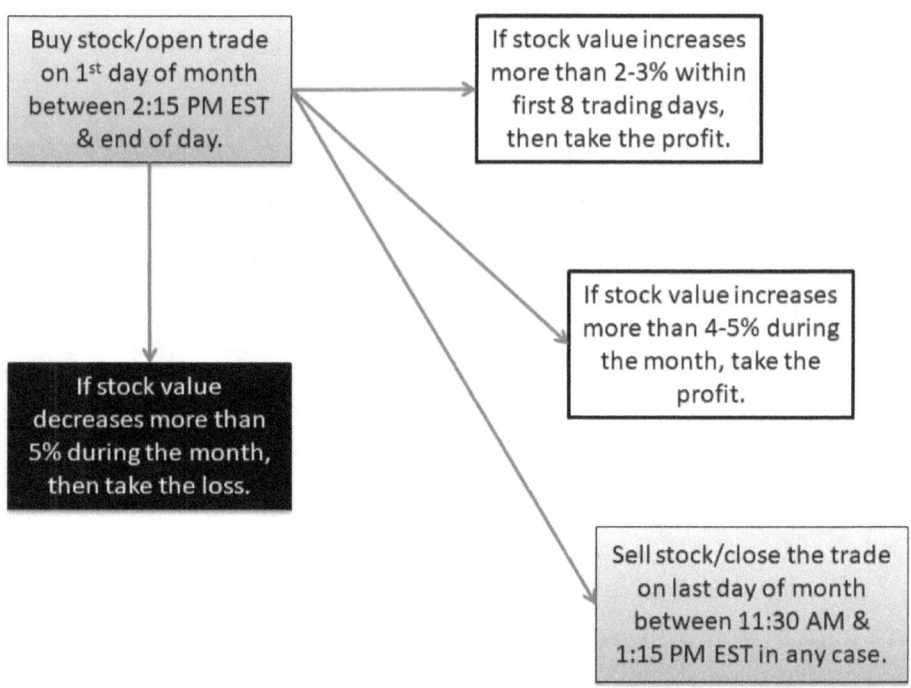

Figure 16: Index profit-loss range

2. **When trading on Sector ETF** (XLE, XLK, XLY, etc.)

Buy the top three sector ETFs on the first day of the month. If there is a 4-5% profit in the first week, take the profit and close the trade. If profit goes up by 6-7% at anytime in the month, take the profit and close the trade.

Set the stop-loss to 5-6% for anytime during that month. Close the trade and accept the loss.

If none of the above scenarios happen at end of the month, close the trade by the last day of the month. That is when either the trade didn't get 5-6% profit or didn't lose 5% of the capital. Close the trade by the last day.

This sector ETFs must be closed at the end of the last trading day of each month. Since our strategy is to buy the top performing sector of each month (which can change every month), it should not carry over to the next month.

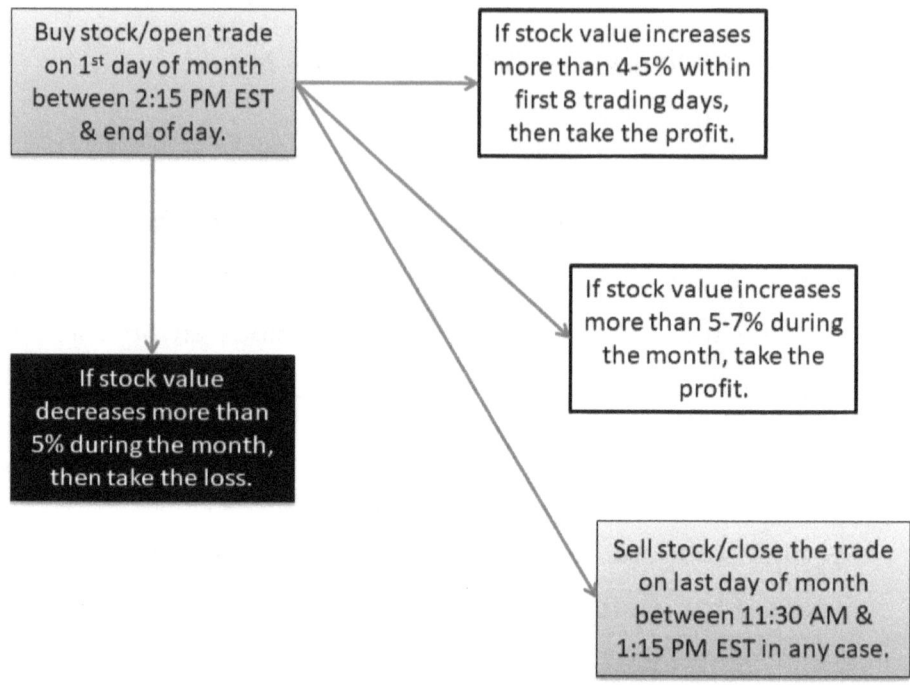

Figure 17: Sector ETF profit-loss range

3. **When trading on Individual Stocks**

Buy the top two stocks of the top five sector ETFs on the first day of the month, as described in the next chapter. If there is a 6% or greater profit in the first week, take the profit and close the trade. If profit goes up by more than 10% at any time in the month, take the profit and close the trade.

Set the stop-loss at 8% for anytime during that month. Close the trade and accept the loss.

If none of the above scenarios happen at end of the month, close the trade by the last day of the month. That is when either the trade didn't get 10% profit, or didn't lose 8% of the capital. Close the trade by month's end.

All ten stocks must be closed by the end of the last trading day of the month. They should not carry over to the next month.

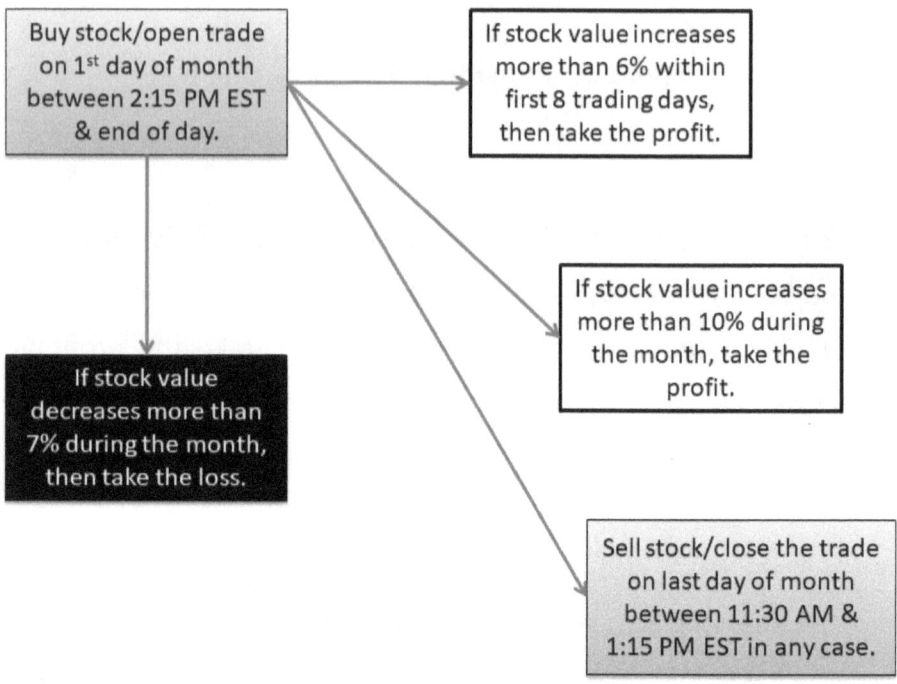

Figure 18: Individual stock profit-loss range

Quarterly

At the beginning of the quarter, find the top performing sector ETFs and stocks, as discussed earlier.

For entering quarterly trade(s), consider buying on a Tuesday, Wednesday, or Thursday rather than on Monday and Friday.

Since our trade timeframe is quarterly, you have some room to grow, and thus attain higher profits.

When closing the trades at the end of the quarter, consider doing this before the third week of the last month in the quarter. There are two reasons for this. First, the third week is options expiration week, so the price can drop when more trade options are in the market. Prices may not bounce back during the last week of the month. The second reason is that mutual fund and institutional managers will sell their non performing, losing stocks, and they might sell their winners as well in order to record a profit. This needs to happen at the end of every quarter, as they must show and prove results for their clients' (positive) quarterly reports.

Stop-Loss: For quarterly timeframe trades, keep the stop-loss set to 5% unless the market is volatile, at which point you can set the stop-loss at 7%; however, don't go below 8%.

Profit Limits: For the profit range, keep it set to 10-15% for stocks, and 7-10% for index and sector ETFs, as discussed in the previous section. When profit reaches 6-8% within the first three weeks, you should close the trade.

Yearly

If you're thinking of trading in the new year, planning for yearly trading, find the top performing sector and stocks, as discussed earlier, using a yearly performance benchmark.

Plan to enter trading during the second week of December, instead of the first week of January. As discussed in the section on quarterly trading, fund and institutional managers will try to close or rebalance their positions for their quarter and yearly reports. But during the third and fourth weeks of December, most fund and institutional managers and traders take a holiday.

At the same time, more and more institutional money will enter the market as these managers deal with New Year's investments and rebalancing activity. Therefore, there is a higher chance of hitting the profit range within the first few weeks of a new calendar year.

Stop-Loss: on yearly trades, don't set the stop-loss below 10%.

Profit Limits: for yearly trading, you can set the profit range at 20-25% for stocks, and 10-15% for index and sector ETFs. If that limit is reached within the first two months, take the profit and wait for a better re-entry time. Most of the time, the price will swing back, giving another opportunity to enter trading.

However, if the stock moves in solid volume with nice demand, hold it for a longer time, you could even allow it to exceed the profit limits discussed above. Leader stocks typically grow more than 50% to 100% yearly, and you don't want to miss the wave.

You must remember the great advice from the legends: *let the winners run, and cut the losers quickly.* This is especially important in terms of the yearly trade timeframe.

STOCKS TO BUY

6. The Best Time to Enter and Exit

As we discussed, profit and loss limits are critical. Obviously, we think that on entering and exiting, we should get a good price.

But you should not chase the price. At the same time, as mutual fund legend Peter Lynch said, we don't want to miss a good trade just because our stop-loss limit/make the trade order was not carried out due to a few pennies' or a dollar's difference.

Instead, we should plan to buy and sell at a specific time of the trading day.

- **BUY**

Always plan to buy during late trading hours, mostly after 2:15 PM EST, but don't forget to place the limit order. 99% of the time, your trade will get filled, even if your buying price has a moderate difference from the market price.

- **SELL**

Don't sell in the first 90 minutes of the market opening, even if the market keeps goes down. Most of the time, it will settle down after 90 minutes from opening. Always try to sell between 11:30 AM EST and1:15 PM EST, but don't try to chase the price, even if the price keeps moving higher. If you keep your limit order in decent territory, 99% of the time it will get filled.

My favorite authors and mentors taught me that the best days to trade are Tuesday, Wednesday, and Thursday, and a good time to trade is from 1:30 PM EST to the close of the market. There are reasons behind this, for example:

- On Monday, the weekend influences may carry over, and the market may be high, low, or volatile. Mondays can also be susceptible to fallout from events of the previous week.

- On Fridays, traders will be in weekend mode, and there may not be enough of a crowd to support the price, supply, or demand. Also, for our own sake, we don't want to spoil our mood, or obsess over a bad trade on the last day of the week. This leads to a tense weekend.

- In the beginning hours of the trading day, the same sorts of factors are at play, and for the rest of the day, traders will be trying to make their fractional profits. Hence, the market can be volatile in the early hours.

Therefore, our strategy is to look for the first and last day of the month, and that can fall on a Monday or a Friday.

However, even if the first or last day of the month comes on a Monday, you are good to trade because as the following section will show, the best time of day to buy is late afternoon.

If the first of the month comes on a Friday, then as per expert advice, we may consider taking it easy and waiting to trade until the following Monday's late trading session.

On the other hand, our trade timeframe is only a month, so it is okay to trade on a Friday. On a Friday, try to buy between 11:00 AM EST and 1:15 PM EST rather than 2:00 PM EST to closing time.

7.It is wise to take a break

Using our strategy, we are making around twenty trades per month. This can make our brains fussy and overactive. We may get feeling that we need to trade every month, and every week. But once in a while, it is also very important to take a break from trading for an extended period of time.

If we are able to schedule some downtime, the mental break will greatly improve our profits.

As William O'Neil pointed out, when a stock drops 50%, it needs to bounce back and grow 100% to catch up.

Historically there are bear markets, or corrections that happen on the bull market. It may not be true every year, but even if a specific time period remains in positive territory, the gains will be very low. It makes sense not to trade at those times.

Consider a scenario in which we have 12%, -15%, 7%, and 6%

profit for the months of January, February, March, and April respectively. If we had avoided trading in February, our total profit would be 25% as opposed to 10%.

The next few statistical tables show the historical drop in market value each week from the beginning of the month. i.e. ,it shows the lowest price reached each week from the start of the month. However, prices could very well have bounced back the next week.

STOCKS TO BUY

In the following tables, please note the legends

LM Close - Last Month Close

7th - The lowest price by the 7th of that month or first week

14th - The lowest price by the 14th of that month or second week

21st - The lowest price by the 21st of that month or third week

28th - The lowest price by the 28th of that month or fourth week

Text in Red - The lowest price in that week. It shows that was the lowest price from the beginning of the month, but that low price is not significant.

Text in Red Box - The lowest price in that week. It shows that was the lowest price from the beginning of the month, but that low is very significant to consider. It could possibly have been avoided.

All prices in U.S. dollars

	2018				
	LM Close	7th	14th	21st	28th
Jan	265.8	2.97	8.12	11.17	15.96
Feb	281.9	-24.27	-24.27	-11.85	-11.5
Mar	271.65	-3.95	2.45	-13.6	-11.85
Apr	263.15	-5.68	-2.15	-0.17	0.48
May	264.51	-1.89	2.41	6.59	7.64
Jun	270.94	2.66	6.19	-1.59	-1.59
Jul					
Aug					
Sep					
Oct					
Nov					
Dec					

STOCKS TO BUY

	2017				
	LM close	7th	14th	21st	28th
Jan	223.53	1.71	2.93	2.38	2.62
Feb	227.53	0.09	1.71	7.19	8.75
Mar	236.47	0.09	0.09	-2.74	-2.85
Apr	235.74	-0.96	-3.23	-2.3	1.43
May	238.08	0.40	0.90	-2.26	1.44
Jun	241.44	1.77	1.20	-0.11	-0.11
Jul	241.8	-1.25	0.39	3.73	5.02
Aug	246.77	0.19	-3.01	-4.06	-2.78
Sep	247.49	-1.43	-0.91	1.59	1.44
Oct	251.23	1.09	2.72	4.06	4.06
Nov	257.15	0.34	-0.71	-0.71	2.61
Dec	265.01	-1.82	20.50	1.50	1.85

	2016				
	LM Close	7th	14th	21st	28th
Jan	203.87	-11.95	-16.06	-18.22	-16.23
Feb	193.72	-8.29	-10.86	-3.94	-1.4
Mar	193.56	4.55	4.84	8.61	9.56
Apr	205.52	-1.57	-1.50	1.93	0.81
May	206.33	-1.36	-1.57	-2.13	-1.12
Jun	209.84	0.43	-2.09	-6.64	-10.24
Jul	209.48	-1.07	3.17	6.35	7.04
Aug	217.12	-1.57	0.52	0.17	0.17
Sep	217.38	-4.10	-4.23	-4.01	-3.14
Oct	216.3	-1.62	-3.29	-3.92	-3.76
Nov	212.55	-4.00	1.56	5.32	7.83
Dec	220.38	-0.81	4.66	4.02	3.15

STOCKS TO BUY

	2015				
	LM Close	7th	14th	21st	28th
Jan	205.54	-5.72	-6.52	-6.52	-6.09
Feb	199.45	2.47	5.18	10.53	11.21
Mar	210.66	-3.16	-6.16	-5.39	-5.39
Apr	206.43	-0.73	1.55	1.52	2.03
May	208.46	-0.42	1.52	3.98	2.24
Jun	211.14	-2.69	-2.72	-2.04	-5.25
Jul	205.89	-1.36	-1.36	2.05	0.85
Aug	210.45	-2.53	-1.79	-23.22	-23.2
Sep	197.54	-5.77	-2.78	-4.67	-9.63
Oct	191.59	0.54	7.70	10.26	13.62
Nov	207.93	2.11	-5.39	-2.46	1.14
Dec	208.69	-3.35	-6.81	-8.67	-5.19

	2014				
	LM Close	7th	14th	21st	28th
Jan	184.69	-2.33	-3	-5.8	-7.34
Feb	178.18	-4.01	1.83	4.84	6.66
Mar	186.29	-1.31	-1.63	-1.71	-1.71
Apr	187.01	-2.67	-5.50	-2.81	-0.72
May	188.31	-1.53	-0.91	-0.91	1.28
Jun	192.68	0.12	0.86	1.61	2.02
Jul	195.72	0.52	0.52	-0.01	1.23
Aug	193.09	-2.06	0.15	2.63	6.10
Sep	200.71	-1.39	-1.58	-4.37	-4.37
Oct	197.02	-4.28	-10.75	-10.75	-4.33
Nov	201.66	-0.59	2.30	2.71	5.45
Dec	207.20	-1.44	-9.29	-9.29	0.27

	2013				
	LM Close	7th	14th	21st	28th
Jan	140.03	5.52	5.52	7.02	9.10
Feb	149.70	-0.16	2.07	0.32	-0.70
Mar	151.61	0.50	3.83	2.75	3.34
Apr	156.67	-1.51	-0.46	-2.53	-0.50
May	159.68	-1.4	3.20	5.63	5.54
Jun	163.45	-2.18	-1.70	-4.88	**-6.39**
Jul	160.42	0.79	3.53	7.10	8.10
Aug	168.71	0.47	-2.88	**-5.38**	**-5.38**
Sep	163.65	0.74	3.98	5.26	5.26
Oct	168.01	-2.53	-2.53	1.69	6.56
Nov	175.79	-0.86	1.17	2.68	4.84
Dec	181.00	-2.06	-2.89	-2.35	1.53

	2012				
	LM Close	7th	14th	21st	28th
Jan	125.50	2.00	2.52	3.84	5.96
Feb	131.32	1.15	3.04	3.24	4.71
Mar	137.02	-2.27	0.02	2.18	2.18
Apr	140.81	-1.02	-4.91	-3.76	-4.02
May	139.87	-4.13	-7.04	-10.13	-8.11
Jun	131.47	-3.37	-0.06	0.51	-0.15
Jul	136.10	-0.61	-2.59	-2.17	-2.17
Aug	137.71	-1.07	2.78	2.95	2.78
Sep	141.16	-0.25	2.35	2.13	2.13
Oct	143.97	0.23	-1.08	-2.95	-2.95
Nov	141.35	-3.31	-5.65	-5.65	-1.02
Dec	142.15	-0.90	-0.05	-2.12	-2.12

	2011				
	LM Close	7th	14th	21st	28th
Jan	125.75	1.23	1.23	1.97	1.99
Feb	128.68	1.81	3.59	2.25	2.25
Mar	133.15	-2.22	-6.97	-6.97	-3.86
Apr	132.59	0.27	-1.13	-2.03	1.05
May	136.43	-2.82	-2.39	-4.48	-4.48
Jun	134.9	-6.48	-7.88	-8.09	-8.09
Jul	131.97	1.84	-1.04	-1.75	-2.64
Aug	129.33	-11.85	-17.07	-16.69	-16.6
Sep	122.22	-6.30	-6.30	-9.36	-9.36
Oct	113.15	-3.22	6.43	7.08	9.90
Nov	125.5	-3.5	-2.34	-8.94	-9.16
Dec	124.99	-0.90	-3.4	-4.7	-0.16

	2010				
	LM Close	7th	14th	21st	28th
Jan	111.44	1.89	2.20	-2.87	-4.05
Feb	107.39	-0.95	-1.50	2.35	2.42
Mar	110.74	1.15	3.53	4.75	5.84
Apr	117.00	0.80	1.77	1.48	1.48
May	118.81	-7.55	-4.92	-11.64	-11.64
Jun	109.37	-3.88	-3.32	-1.95	-6.15
Jul	103.22	-1.02	3.44	3.44	6.24
Aug	110.27	1.95	-1.96	-5.04	-5.04
Sep	105.31	3.15	5.1	7.18	7.19
Oct	114.13	-0.38	2.41	2.6	4.22
Nov	118.49	0.04	-0.33	-0.33	-0.04
Dec	118.49	2.52	4.79	5.61	7.11

	2009				
	LM Close	7th	14th	21st	28th
Jan	90.67	-1.58	-6.30	-10.10	-7.92
Feb	82.83	-0.25	-0.07	-8.90	-8.90
Mar	73.93	-5.13	-5.82	1.93	6.67
Apr	79.52	1.54	3.01	3.91	5.02
May	87.42	0.47	1.26	1.29	1.60
Jun	92.53	1.12	-0.89	-3.18	-3.25
Jul	91.95	-3.95	-3.99	1.16	3.60
Aug	98.81	1.08	0.92	-0.50	4.15
Sep	102.46	-2.64	0.48	1.99	1.99
Oct	105.59	-3.10	1.02	-1.18	-2.03
Nov	103.56	0.76	5.47	5.87	6.01
Dec	109.94	-0.33	-0.33	0.24	1.79

	2008				
	LM Close	7th	14th	21st	28th
Jan	146.21	-7.30	-9.23	-14.15	-15.49
Feb	137.37	-4.32	-4.30	-2.58	-3.55
Mar	133.82	-4.11	-5.82	-5.52	-2.31
Apr	131.97	3.86	0.96	1.27	5.75
May	138.26	0.64	0.64	-0.62	-0.62
Jun	140.35	-4.06	-6.41	-12.82	-12.82
Jul	127.98	-3.19	-6.99	-6.99	-4.34
Aug	126.83	-1.84	1.74	0.16	0.19
Sep	128.79	-5.57	-6.69	-12.18	-12.80
Oct	115.99	-25.29	-27.49	-28.95	-32.04
Nov	96.83	-5.97	-11.01	-21.38	-11.8
Dec	90.09	-7.98	-2.15	-3.93	-3.93

STOCKS TO BUY

	2007				
	LM Close	7th	14th	21st	28th
Jan	142.21	-1.67	-1.14	-0.08	-0.08
Feb	143.75	0.19	-0.30	-4.25	-4.25
Mar	140.93	-3.58	-2.68	-2.40	0.89
Apr	142.00	0.16	2.02	4.70	6.06
May	148.29	0.38	1.29	2.28	2.77
Jun	**153.32**	-4.22	-3.67	-5.03	-5.03
Jul	150.43	1.36	0.49	-5.32	-5.32
Aug	145.72	-1.92	-4.68	-4.68	-2.00
Sep	147.59	-1.52	-1.80	0.51	3.80
Oct	152.58	1.20	1.20	-2.91	-2.04
Nov	154.65	-9.51	-10.95	-12.97	-13.7
Dec	148.66	-2.30	-1.49	-3.59	-1.36

Learning from SPY (S&P 500's ETF) statistics

From the above data, it is clear that the most dangerous period to trade is from the last week of January to the first couple of weeks of February. Also, the first three weeks of October are not showing of positive probability. Therefore, it is good to consider not trading during these periods. If we had the stop-loss orders set as we discussed earlier, those stop-loss trades could have been executed in these "danger" weeks. This could negatively affect our trades, and overall strategy.

Despite positive trends during these times, the range is very narrow. If we can avoid trading in those particular weeks and months, we will be better off in the long run.

8. Fifty : Thirty : Twenty (50:30:20)

There are strategies to trading, such as: equal weighted, equal dollar allocation, weight based on stock size, or trends. Fund and institutional managers hedge their positions with index, sector ETFs, and options to maximize profit.

50:30:20 is a strategy that trades a combination of S&P 500 index ETF (SPY), top performing sector ETFs, and top performing individual stocks every month.

Here is how the allocation ratio **50:30:20** works:

The top two performing stocks in the top five performing sectors : the top three performing sector ETFs : SPY.

For example, if you have twenty thousand dollars worth of capital, you can allocate it in the ratio of 50:30:20. With that, you will have ten thousand for stocks, which makes two thousand dollars to invest in each stock; six thousand goes to sector ETFs, which gives two thousand for each sector ETF, and finally, four thousand on the S&P 500 index, ETF SPY.

This gives safety, diversification, and a focused profit margin. If individual stocks perform poorly, then the sector ETFs can help move the portfolio to a more positive territory. When all three sectors of the ETFs go against the odds, the other better-performing sector can lead the SPY. That equalizes the loss using our better performing sector ETF and or stocks.

If all of them do well, we can definitely beat the S&P 500 performance by 200% to 300% or more every month.

Covered Call: If you have more than enough capital to split as per the ratio, sell a call option with 100 stocks or ETFs, which then creates a better cushion for loss and profit margin. This can maximize the opportunity to beat the S&P 500 every month and over the year.

I have tried many systems and strategies. This one works consistently and is a safe and easy way to trade and follow with minimal time spent each month. You can also try make adjustments to the system, as you will see in the case study in the next chapter.

9. A Case Study of (50:30:20) Trades in 2018

In this case study, the 50:30:20 strategy is tested from January to June 2018. For this six-month period, twenty thousand dollars was invested each month in the S&P 500 ETF SPY, in the three best performing sectors, and the top two individual stocks in the five best performing sectors. Each month's profit was not reinvested. The performance percentage does not include the dividends that were paid out for that month or quarter.

Stocks are bought the first day of each month, between from 1:15 PM and 4:00 PM EST, with the limit order in place.

SPY is sold if it makes 2-3% profit in the first week, and 5-6% any time, to book the profit. However, if the loss is 5% at any time, it is sold out to minimize losses.

The three best performing ETFs are closed if there is an increase of 3-5% within the first week or 6-7% at any time, in order to book the profit, and are closed when the value goes down by 5%, to cut losses.

The ten individual stocks are closed if price increases 5-7% within the first week, or 10% or more at any time, to book the profit. They are closed when they go down by 5%, to cut losses.

On the total profit calculation, $20 commission fees are deducted, assuming $10 for buying and $10 for selling the trade.

When profit or loss limits are reached with the closing price on any day, the stocks will be closed the next day, between 11:00 AM to 1:30 PM EST with a limit order.

In this case study, February is not avoided, as we discussed in Chapter 7. This is to test how the result could have been changed if we could have avoided.

To get a better view of the following tables in mobile, switch to landscape orientation.

Profits were not reinvested and losses are not adjusted, assuming that every month we had twenty thousand dollars to invest.

You will see 50:30:20's overall performance was 3.26%, but if February was avoided, then it would be 10.13%, whereas S&P 500's performance was -1.26%.

All prices in U.S. dollars.

January 2018

S&P 500 Performance: 2.30%

Tick.	Sec.	Buy Price	Sell Price	Profit	Date Sold
SPY		268.12	281.68	183.40	23
XLE	Eng.	72.95	77.96	115.27	24
XLY	Cons. Disc.	99.85	107.60	135.00	24
XLI	Ind.	75.76	80.13	93.62	30
Total Sectors Profit		343.89		Avg. No. Days	24
SPY +Total Sectors Profit		527.29		Avg. No. Days	23
HAL	Eng.	49.35	53.43	61.60	13
HP	Eng.	64.70	69.82	56.80	14
DFS	Fin.	76.64	80.85	34.73	30
SYF	Fin.	38.72	40.11	16.14	24
LUV	Ind.	66.00	60.30	-105.50	25
ARNC	Ind.	27.52	29.52	52.00	6
DISCA	Cons. Disc.	22.83	24.15	38.08	13
KSS	Cons. Disc.	55.95	64.00	124.90	17
NUE	Mat.	66.30	67.12	-7.70	31
FCX	Mat.	19.55	19.30	-32.75	31
Total Individual Stocks Profit			238.3	Avg. No. Days	18
Sectors + Individual Stocks Profit			582.19	Avg. No. Days	20
SPY + Sectors + Ind. Stocks Profit			765.59	Avg. No. Days	20
50:30:20 performance of this			3.83%		

month	
S&P 500 Cumulative performance	2.30%
50:30:20 Cumulative performance	3.83%

February 2018
S&P 500 Performance: -3.35%

Tick.	Sec.	Buy Price	Sell Price	Profit	Date Sold
SPY		281.00	260.00	-314.00	6
XLY	Cons. Discr.	105.43	101.14	-101.51	5
XLF	Fin.	29.72	29.35	-44.79	28
XLK	Tech.	68.23	69.18	7.55	28
Total Sectors Profit		-138.75		Avg. No. Days 19	
SPY +Total Sectors Profit		-452.75		Avg. No. Days 16	
AAP	Cons. Disc.	114.52	108.00	-78.68	13
DG	Cons. Disc.	102.00	96.37	-76.30	6
MCO	Fin.	162.65	156.00	-59.90	6
BLK	Fin.	563.12	525.00	-96.24	6
STX	Tech.	54.00	49.00	-115.00	6
AMD	Tech.	13.35	11.47	-161.00	6
CAH	Health.	69.06	69.00	-20.84	28
HUM	Health.	278.00	263.67	-77.32	8
TDG	Ind.	314.00	270.00	-152.00	6
GD	Ind.	226.00	210.00	-84.00	6
Total Individual Stocks Profit			-921.28	Avg. No. Days 8	
Sectors + Individual Stocks Profit			- 1060.03	Avg. No. Days 11	
SPY + Sectors + Ind. Stocks			-	Avg. No. Days	

Profit	1374.03	10
50:30:20 performance of this month	-6.87%	
S&P 500 Cumulative performance	1.42%	
50:30:20 Cumulative performance	-3.04%, if February avoided 3.83%	

STOCKS TO BUY

March 2018
S&P 500 Performance: -0.99%

Tick.	Sec.	Buy Price	Sell Price	Profit	Date Sold
SPY		266.60	279.00	166.00	12
XLK	Tech.	67.00	71.02	100.60	13
XLU	Util.	49.00	50.60	45.60	29
XLY	Cons. Disc.	102.35	107.00	73.00	13
Total Sectors Profit			219.20	Avg. No. Days 17	
SPY +Total Sectors Profit			385.20	Avg. No. Days 16	
QRVO	Tech.	79.12	86.18	71.78	13
eBay	Tech.	42.12	43.91	22.96	18
SRE	Util.	107.05	110.82	13.93	29
FE	Util.	32.16	34.08	39.52	29
TRIP	Cons. Disc.	39.52	44.30	99.50	15
UAA	Cons. Disc.	16.10	17.15	45.10	5
RTN	Ind.	210.32	213.22	-5.50	29
NOC	Ind.	338.00	349.23	13.69	29
PGR	Fin.	57.33	62.18	62.45	21
AJG	Fin.	68.00	71.87	38.05	12
Total Individual Stocks Profit			401.48	Avg. No. Days 19	
Sectors + Individual Stocks Profit			620.68	Avg. No. Days 19	
SPY + Sectors + Ind. Stocks Profit			786.68	Avg. No. Days 18	

50:30:20 performance of this month	3.93%
S&P 500 Cumulative performance	-1.75%
50:30:20 Cumulative performance	0.89%, if February avoided 7.72%

April 2018
S&P 500 Performance: 0.75%

Tick.	Sec.	Buy Price	Sell Price	Profit	Date Sold
SPY		256.00	266.20	163.20	6
XLRE	Real Es.	30.60	30.73	-11.55	30
XLU	Util.	50.00	51.75	50.00	30
XLE	Eng.	65.50	73.65	232.65	13
Total Sectors Profit			271.10	Avg. No. Days	22
SPY +Total Sectors Profit			414.30	Avg. No. Days	18
EQR	Real Es.	60.75	62.12	1.92	30
DRE	Real Es.	25.60	27.50	54.10	30
NRG	Util.	30.10	31.25	17.95	30
NEE	Util.	161.50	164.35	-2.90	30
MPC	Eng.	71.32	79.20	90.32	18
ANDV	Eng.	99.83	112.12	102.90	11
HRL	Cons. Stap.	33.40	36.40	70.00	5
EL	Cons. Stap.	147.12	149.76	-1.52	30
HRG	Mat.	15.35	11.25	-286.50	27
EGN	Mat.	60.82	68.25	98.88	19
Total Individual Stocks Profit			145.15	Avg. No. Days	21
Sectors + Individual Stocks Profit			416.25	Avg. No. Days	21
SPY + Sectors + Ind. Stocks Profit			559.45	Avg. No. Days	20

50:30:20 performance of this month	2.80%
S&P 500 Cumulative performance	-1.24%
50:30:20 Cumulative performance	3.69%, if February avoided 10.56%

May 2018
S&P 500 Performance: 2.68%

Tick.	Sector	Buy Price	Sell Price	Profit	Date Sold
SPY		263.56	271.50	99.10	31
XLE	Eng.	72.96	77.32	97.72	15
XLV	Health	81.88	83.02	7.36	31
XLY	Cons. Disc.	103.11	105.83	31.68	31
Total Sectors Profit			136.76	Avg. No. Days 25	
SPY +Total Sectors Profit			235.86	Avg. No. Days 26	
NFX	Eng.	29.84	29.15	-43.46	31
BHGE	Eng.	35.48	35.17	-28.68	31
HSIC	Health	76.51	71.00	-91.63	30
HUM	Health	293.70	295.16	-15.62	31
ULTA	Cons. Disc	249.87	253.25	-6.48	31
M	Cons. Disc	30.55	34.52	111.01	17
AES	Util.	12.18	12.75	26.74	31
AWK	Util.	86.43	84.57	-42.32	31
MOS	Mat.	26.81	29.00	61.03	31
ECL	Mat.	146.83	143.80	-41.21	31
Total Individual Stocks Profit			-70.62	Avg. No. Days 29	
Sectors + Individual Stocks Profit			66.14	Avg. No. Days 28	
SPY + Sectors + Ind. Stocks Profit			165.24	Avg. No. Days 28	
50:30:20 performance of this month			0.83%		

S&P 500 Cumulative performance	1.16%
50:30:20 Cumulative performance	4.52%, if February avoided 11.39%

STOCKS TO BUY

June 2018					
S&P 500 Performance: -0.42%					
Tick.	Sec.	Buy Price	Sell Price	Profit	Date Sold
SPY		273.43	273.12	-24.65	29
XLK	Tech.	70.93	69.92	-48.28	29
XLI	Ind.	75.14	72.95	-79.13	22
XLE	Eng.	76.25	76.12	-23.38	29
Total Sectors Profit				-150.79	Avg. Num. Days 26
SPY +Total Sectors Profit				-175.44	Avg. Num. Days 26
MU	Tech.	57.94	61.95	48.17	11
AMD	Tech.	14.27	15.65	76.60	12
EXPD	Ind.	75.74	73.84	-44.70	29
DE	Ind.	153.70	141.02	-108.76	26
MRO	Eng.	21.32	21.26	-22.82	29
DVN	Eng.	41.25	44.32	53.68	29
VMC	Mat.	129.65	129.52	-21.04	29
MLM	Mat.	225.58	225.42	-20.64	29
HST	Real Es.	21.86	21.12	-54.04	29
EXR	Real Es.	96.44	100.15	17.10	29
Total Individual Stocks Profit				-76.45	Avg. No. Days 24
Sectors + Individual Stocks Profit				-227.24	Avg. No. Days 25
SPY + Sectors + Ind. Stocks Profit				-251.89	Avg. No. Days 25
50:30:20 performance of this month				-1.26%	
S&P 500 Cumulative				1.28%	

performance	
50:30:20 Cumulative performance	3.26%, if February avoided 10.13%

STOCKS TO BUY

10. Preparing mentally and emotionally for a better trade

Trading is also an emotional game.

In order to make profitable trades, it is very important to carry out rigorous technical and fundamental analyses of the market. You must also keep learning new strategies and algorithms. Always be on the lookout for good books on new techniques, and strategies.

At the same time, you need to practice or become 'seasoned' regarding the physiological and psychological perspectives of trading. Again, keep an eye out for good books on new techniques and strategies in these fields.

Trading experts like Mark Douglas (his best work is *Trading in the Zone*), and Alexander Elder (his best guide is *Trading for a Living*) give their advice and lessons, and a new vision, in the form of books. It is also good practice to attend classes given by experts and to follow their blogs to gain both practice and knowledge.

However, you are the one who must apply and execute the strategy and practice you have learned every time.

Here are a few tips that may be helpful.

Maintaining a calm mind plays a very important role in successful, profitable trading.

Even if you lose a trade, you need to have a positive mindset, and think, "I had a good trade," rather than feeling, "I have been beaten, or fooled". If you have the "I was beaten or fooled" mindset, then you will only experience that negative reaction over and over again. Losing a trade is not the responsibility of others, or a fault of the market. It happens because of your own actions and behavior, so take full responsibility and accountability for your trades, actions, and attitude.

- Listen keenly for important signals over the extremely noisy space of the market—just as you would when driving in traffic during peak hours. There will be so much going on when you reach home or the office that you will forget all the regular noise you encountered on the way. But you will no doubt remember a bad accident or a fire engine siren.

- Chasing may feel good, but severe damage may result as if you are chasing the price —e.g., chasing a police car.

- Mastery takes time. Like a growing child learning to walk, until you gain experience and achieve success, just keep practicing. Somebody may laugh at you, or you may feel pain, or even shame if you are overwhelmed by losses in the early phases of your trading life. In such situations, pause for a moment, but don't quit. By that time, you need to ask yourself if it's worth it to sit while the others learn how to walk?

- During the pause, analyze your mistakes. Most important, make sure you are not betting with emergency savings funds, money needed for everyday necessities, or worse, borrowed capital. In such cases, think carefully; pretend that you don't have any money to trade. Keep watching the market, but do only "paper trades."

- No egos— only learning! Practice zero ego to deal with your losses or successes. Don't be mad at the market or people who defeat you on a trade. Also, do not feel jealousy towards people you know who have traded successfully. They are defeating you and/or winning because they have learned or applied better skills. Profit from your own trading successes, and also learn well from your losses.

- Say no to Buy and Hold: If you are planning to buy and hold then it's better to go for boring but solid companies that pay a nice dividend. Don't rely on trending or beaten stocks. Those stocks will give only negative results.

- No Day Trading: When day trading, you will most likely succumb to rushed and irrational behavior that leads to losses. Even if you make money, there are no guarantees you will keep it because your brain power will burn out very quickly. There are a few exceptional day traders: they are all very mature professionals who keep their emotions in check. If you read their blogs or words of advice, you discover that even though they day trade, they only do so a few days a month. Most days, they keep watching the market and practicing their skills.

- Brainpower: Keeping control of your emotions and supporting your brainpower is important. Add coconut oil and avocado to your breakfast; they can boost your brain power. Stress is the number one brainpower burner, so don't watch TV or read blogs constantly. Instead, take a break and walk 10-15 minutes every hour.

- Try to avoid trading on Fridays and Monday mornings: When you make a bad trade on Friday, you will be upset all weekend and that will spoil family time. If you do trade on Friday, try to wind down and enjoy the weekend. Watch a movie, have a couple of drinks, and spend time with the family and kids. That is more important than the trade. Usually on Monday mornings, the market needs to digest and react to events of the previous week, so trading on a Monday may also lead to bad results.

In short, enjoy your life and your weekends as much as you enjoy your trades and investments.

STOCKS TO BUY

RAJENDRAN SELVARAJ

Best of LUCK for your PROFITS and EXCITEMENT

Summary

- Market and sector uptrend is your friend; crowd psychology does work.

- Sector ETFs are the better choice for diversified and focused trading.

- The sector and stocks leaders in the trend will lead the index as well.

- The SMA (simple moving averages) chart can be used as a tool to identify the trends.

- Every month's uptrending stocks and ETFs can be viewed online, showing their past month's performance.

- Profit and loss limits and choosing the best time for entry and exit will maximize profit and reduce losses.

- The odds of beating the S&P 500 are high when single-worst month (or week) trades are avoided.

- The 50:30:20 is a safe and diversified strategy for getting a better performance than the S&P 500.

A seasoned, calm mind along with controlled emotions has a higher probability of winning trades than a fussy mind and panic.

A favor from you…

Thank you for purchasing my book.

Please take a few minutes of your time to write a review if you feel this book is helpful or enjoyable reading. You can drop me an email at:<u>selvraj@yahoo.com</u>.

Your feedback helps me a lot in terms of updating the content for my upcoming work. I greatly appreciate your reviews and comments.

Month's weekly low worksheet

	Year				
	LM Close	7th	14th	21st	28th
Jan					
Feb					
Mar					
Apr					
May					
Jun					
Jul					
Aug					
Sep					
Oct					
Nov					
Dec					

50:30:20 worksheet

Month Year					
S&P 500 Performance:					
Tick.	Sec.	Buy Price	Sell Price	Profit	Date Sold
SPY					
Total Sectors Profit				Avg. Num. Days	
SPY +Total Sectors Profit				Avg. Num. Days	
Total Individual Stocks Profit				Avg. Num. Days	
Sectors + Individual Stocks Profit				Avg. Num. Days	
SPY + Sectors + Ind. Stocks Profit				Avg. Num. Days	
50:30:20 performance of this					

month
S&P 500 Cumulative performance
50:30:20 Cumulative performance

References

- The Neatest Little Guide to Stock Market by Jason Kelly

- The Four Pillars of Investing: Lessons for Building a Winning Portfolio by William J. Bernstein

- Common Stocks and Uncommon Profits by Philip A. Fisher

- The Intelligent Investor by Benjamin Graham

- The Seven Rules of Wall Street: Crash-Tested Investment Strategies That Beat the Market by Sam Stovall

- How to Make Money in Stocks: A Winning System in Good Times and Bad by William J. O'Neil

- One Up On Wall Street: How To Use What You Already Know To Make Money by Peter Lynch

- Rule #1: The Simple Strategy for Successful Investing in Only 15 Minutes a Week! by Phil Town

- Buy High, Sell Higher: Why Buy-And-Hold Is Dead And Other Investing Lessons from CNBC's "The Liquidator" by Joe Terranova

- *Standard & Poor's Sector Investing: How to Buy The Right Stock in The Right Industry at The Right Time by Sam Stovall*

- *What Works on Wall Street: A Guide to the Best-Performing Investment Strategies of All Time by James P. O'Shaughnessy*

- *The Only Three Questions That Still Count: Investing By Knowing What Others Don't by Ken Fisher*

- *Learn to Trade Momentum Stocks by Matthew R. Kratter*

- *Rocket Stocks: Learn to Profit from the Stock Market's Biggest Winners by Matthew R. Kratter*

- *Moving Averages 101: Incredible Signals That Will Make You Money in the Stock Market by Steve Burns*

- *Trading Habits: 39 of the World's Most Powerful Stock Market Rules by Steve Burns, Holly Burns*

- *The Little Book That Beats the Market by Joel Greenblatt*

- *Stocks for the Long Run 5/E: The Definitive Guide to Financial Market Returns & Long-Term Investment Strategies by Jeremy J. Siegel*

- *The Future for Investors: Why the Tried and the True Triumphs Over the Bold and the New by Jeremy J. Siegel*

- *Buy and Hedge: The 5 Iron Rules for Investing Over the Long Term by Jay Pestrichelli and Wayne Ferbert*

STOCKS TO BUY

- *The Complete TurtleTrader: How 23 Novice Investors Became Overnight Millionaires by Michael W. Covel*

- *Dual Momentum Investing: An Innovative Strategy for Higher Returns with Lower Risk by Gary Antonacci*

- *The 3% Signal: The Investing Technique That Will Change Your Life Paperback by Jason Kelly*

- *The Most Important Thing Illuminated: Uncommon Sense for the Thoughtful Investor by Howard Marks and Paul Johnson*

- *Trading in the Zone: Master the Market with Confidence, Discipline, and a Winning Attitude by Mark Douglas*

- *Trading for a Living, Study Guide: Psychology, Trading Tactics, Money Management by Alexander Elder*

- *https://finviz.com/*

- *https://finance.yahoo.com*

- *https://google.com/finance*

- *https://www.marketwatch.com/*

- *https://www.investopedia.com*

- *http://www.sectorspdr.com*

ABOUT THE AUTHOR

Rajendran Selvaraj is a software developer working for a Fortune 500 company. He has also worked as a software consultant for various industry leaders.

Raj has been a trader for more than a decade. He is always excited to learn new trading and investing strategies.

Raj believes that ideas and concepts are to be shared. Sharing thoughts with others is often equivalent to learning something new, and it results in broader knowledge and enriched experience. Raj always shares and teaches his ideas and thoughts.

www.ingramcontent.com/pod-product-compliance
Lightning Source LLC
Chambersburg PA
CBHW030641220526
45463CB00004B/1601